TENNIS AND THE SKILL OF RELAXATION

Daryl D. Fisher

Philosopher Coach Press

Warning: Before embarking on the exercises suggested in this book, a reader should first consult with his or her physician who can make recommendations about the advisability of these suggested exercises based upon each reader's medical history and current medical conditions. This publication contains the opinions and ideas of its author. It is intended to provide helpful and informative material on the subject matter covered. The author and publisher disclaim any responsibility for any liability, loss, or risk, personal or otherwise, which is incurred as a consequence directly or indirectly, of the use and application of any of the contents of this book.

Published in the United States by Philosopher Coach Press
First Edition
ISBN 978-1-959494-00-3

In order to purchase copies of this book, or inquire about Daryl Fisher's consulting services or speaking, please visit https://darylfisher.com/

CONTENTS

1

THE IMPORTANCE OF RELAXATION

"The best way to achieve wisdom is to learn the big ideas that underlie reality..."
–Charlie Munger

"What lies behind us and what lies before us are tiny matters compared to what lies within us."
–Ralph Waldo Emerson

"What I improve a lot is to don't take the pressure, just to play relaxed. That's why I show a great level, because I feel like I have no pressure. I enjoy. I'm playing relaxed."
–Carlos Alcaraz

Take a moment to remember your best experiences playing tennis. Your strokes were effortless. Your movement was easy. You likely noticed better-than-normal control and power. You felt *relaxed.*

In order for you to enjoy such on-court experiences more frequently, and even routinely, you will need to invest some time in understanding what happens when they occur. What does being "relaxed" mean for tennis players? Definitions can be challenging in general, but relaxation is particularly problematic given how widely its meaning varies across contexts. For the context of tennis, which requires physical action, think of relaxation as the minimal amount of muscular tension necessary to perform an action and no more. Roger Federer, one of the greatest players of all time, provided the perfect example of being relaxed while striking a tennis ball. This is not to say that he didn't expend effort; rather, he used *only* the tension that was required.

Tennis requires precise coordination and timing, which is facilitated by an optimal balance of muscular tension. Relaxation contributes to your results by removing excess tension and effort. In contrast to your best experiences, you have probably also noticed that when relaxation has eluded you a performance drop has followed.

Now for the weird part. As important as relaxation is for the highest levels of one's tennis ability, rarely does anyone discuss relaxation as a skill to study and improve. In fact, for many players, coaches, teachers, and academics, relaxation is the most over-looked fundamental in tennis development. Rather than dismiss relaxation as largely beyond our control, attention to relaxation can significantly enhance the way tennis is played, coached, taught, and studied.

Tennis could benefit from such a boost. Sadly, for all of the sport's new participants over time, *about the same number stop playing*. Reasons for stopping include both the difficulty of the sport and injuries, but attention to relaxation can make learning the sport more fun and simultaneously reduce players' injuries. More people could enjoy tennis, and they could play for more years, if they just learned to relax. As an example,

Federer's physical ease while playing put comparatively less stress on his body over the years, and his rate of injury was correspondingly lower than most. He played in 65 consecutive Grand Slam tournaments — over 16 years without missing one! Relaxation can truly help tennis live up to its designation as "the sport for a lifetime."

For those of us who love tennis, and who passionately strive to both improve and help others improve, not giving relaxation considerable attention is oddly narrow-sighted. While we nitpick what we see in slow-motion videos of great players, we often overlook the great players' distinct lack of excess tension. *This is even after some of the greatest players have told us how valuable relaxation is.* For example, Pete Sampras has praised Federer's ease as one of his greatest competitive assets. Sampras is certainly a credible source on the topic; unsurprisingly, a significant factor for his own success was also an effortless-looking game, particularly his serve. Many of us recognize the truth of what Sampras has said about Federer…yet why do we give that indicator of success such little attention? When Sampras tells us something about a contributing factor to success, and specifically the success of Federer, should we not pay utmost attention for what it could do for us?

If you are a tennis player, no matter what your current skill level, learning more about relaxation might be what you need to improve. You will soon discover that the skill of relaxation is intertwined with every other aspect of tennis. Relaxation can help you develop more efficient technique, as well as more control and more power. It will likely help you play with less fatigue and with fewer injuries. All of this, in turn, offers a chance to play tennis with greater enjoyment.

If you are a teacher, coach, or academic, learning more about relaxation will broaden your understanding of the countless movements made by the greatest players. Some movements are crucial fundamentals, but others are idiosyncratic and meaningless. Tennis will always remain complicated, but your widened vision that includes an understanding of the skills of relaxation will enable clearer and simpler communication of all fundamental skills. Understanding relaxation will enable you to help others increase their potential for continual improvement, which is critical to the ongoing popularity of our sport.

2

AWARENESS OF TENSION

"The key to growth is the introduction of higher dimensions of consciousness into our awareness."
–Lao Tzu

"What is necessary to change a person is to change his awareness of himself."
–Abraham Maslow

"It's in our hands."
–Björk

As a child, I recall noticing that my handwriting changed depending on how tightly I held my pen or pencil. When my hand was more relaxed, my handwriting looked much nicer, and was more pleasant to create. Try it. Write a sentence or two while gripping your pen or pencil tightly, and then try re-writing what you wrote, but with a more relaxed grip. Compare the penmanship, and the general writing experience, for each.

If you're able to adjust the tension of your grip as you hold your pen or pencil, then you just did what's necessary to adjust tension in the rest of your body. Adjusting tension starts with awareness, and it can be easy.

Well, perhaps it *could* be easy if we weren't so inclined to ignore tension. In fact, we often ignore tension even when it causes pain or exhaustion. At times, I've squeezed a pen but haven't noticed the discomfort of excess tension until my hand was exhausted. Why did the unnecessary tension go unnoticed? Was I so focused on what I was writing that I had no remaining awareness for the tension in my hand? Or had I just grown accustomed to excessive tension, and no longer noticed it? Regardless, this tendency similarly resurfaces when I play tennis, and over years of observing other tennis players, I've concluded that others share this tendency. It is not that we don't want to sense tension, but we just don't for some reason.

Our inability to spot tension leaves us unprepared to address it. How can we solve a problem that we generally ignore? We should instead foster our awareness of tension as an independent skill that can be improved.

When you deliberately varied tension while writing, the tension that changed was specifically in your hand. Knowing where to look made changing the tension easier. But tennis is a complex game, involving the entire body and mind. So, for tennis, where should you look?

Believe it or not, tennis players should also look for excess tension in the hands. In fact, one of the more useful solutions for tennis players hoping to maximize their potential is relaxing their hands. *Hand tension significantly affects your tennis game.*

Players and coaches typically consider the place where our skin meets the tennis racquet to select a grip (Continental, Eastern forehand, etc.), but, beyond that, the hands are often forgotten. We are challenged to give any attention to body parts that do not perceptibly move. We neglect to notice that the muscles in the hands tense and release during tennis play.

Alternatively, if a body part clearly moves, or doesn't move when it should, excess tension is more quickly noticeable. For example, if your legs stiffen up when you try to move them, you'll likely notice that excess tension fairly quickly. Noticing the tension then allows you to adjust it.

The subtler the movement, however, the less likely the tension will be noticed. Players regularly tense their hands excessively without anyone noticing, and some never become consciously aware of the excess tension in their hands unless it's brought to their attention. After I once told a student about the value of relaxing the hands, he remarked, "Until we talked about relaxation, I didn't notice I was squeezing the sh** out of the racquet!"

Any tension that you experience is at least partly mental, but if you're convinced that your tension is *only* mental and that addressing physical (hand) tension is therefore a waste of time, consider that as you develop an awareness of tension, you will instead begin to notice that different types of tension are interconnected. For this reason, if you feel mental tension, then it has likely already surfaced somewhere in your muscles — and vice versa.

That mental tension raises blood pressure and heart rates is long-established, but the converse notion that physical actions influence mental tension is now similarly accepted. Research has shown, for example, that manipulating facial muscles, as when faking a smile or even holding a pencil within teeth, can impact mood by triggering the chemical release of dopamine and serotonin. Another study has even shown that one's mood can be positively affected by using Botox to paralyze the facial muscles used for frowning.

Now consider Rafael Nadal saying, after losing to Fabio Fognini at the 2015 US Open, "You want to hit the forehand here, and you hit the forehand there. It's because you don't have the mentally relax. You are not enough relaxed in your mind to do what you used to do." Not being relaxed affected what Nadal could achieve, and though he refers here to the mental side of being relaxed, the physical aspect of relaxation is inextricably intertwined. His mental tension affected his physical results. Even for Nadal, a master of mental and physical toughness, one manifestation of tension inevitably entails the other.

To be clear, this book doesn't intend to promote Botox or encourage smiling for no good reason. It simply encourages awareness of tension for the sake of playing better tennis. Moving forward, since mental and physical tensions are interconnected, there's actually little need to distinguish between them. When it comes to tennis, any closer detail isn't really that helpful. We can simply explore tension, with the sole focus being on what amount is optimal.

Given that mental and physical tensions are intertwined, consider three options for identifying tension: one in which you're to identify and pinpoint mental tension, another in which you're to identify and pinpoint overall physical tension, and a third in which you're to identify and pinpoint physical tension *in a specific area of your body*. Mental tension is really difficult to pinpoint. You might think of things that cause you to be tense, such as certain competitive situations, but it's difficult to *locate* the mental tension associated with those moments. Next, overall physical tension might be easier to recognize, but difficult to evaluate with specificity. After all, you've got a lot of muscles. Last, regarding a specific area of your body, how much tension do you notice, for example, in your hands? You will likely find that identifying tension in this way is markedly easier than the first two.

There are countless ways to develop your relaxation skills beyond those presented in this book. Try to keep an open-minded approach to the topic of relaxation, and in this way you will open yourself to countless useful ideas from other cultures, eras, and disciplines. While such an array of options may seem overwhelming, the upside is that we can enjoy exploration and improvement for our entire tennis-playing lives. We'll never run out of information on the topic of relaxation.

No matter how you choose to address excess tension, you should always start with *awareness*. And unless you have a better idea, why not start with an awareness of hand tension? Hand tension is simple and effective. While our goal as tennis players is to decrease tension in general, excess tension typically collects in a player's hands, similar to excess tension collecting in a computer user's neck and shoulders. If you discover that tension seems to collect most often in another part (or parts) of your body, consider lending more attention to that part(s). Again, years of observing suggests that nearly all tennis players should give more awareness to their hands — and in most cases, that just means giving more than zero awareness.

There's a chance that awareness of hand tension alone will change the way you approach the game. In fact, such awareness may encourage a number of surprising revelations and initiate a range of additional benefits. Hand tension is quite relevant when it comes to control, power, technique, rate of improvement, and more.

Read on.

3

MORE CONTROL

"Life itself is but what you deem it."
–Marcus Aurelius

In the same way that beauty is in the eye of the beholder, control depends on your own experience of it. You have to feel it for yourself. To that end, try the following experiment while playing tennis: Aim for a target while intentionally squeezing your racquet handle tightly, then aim for the same target while relaxed. (Keep in mind that "relaxed" in the context of playing tennis simply means that there is no excess strain or tension.) You might not hit the target in either attempt, but perhaps the contrast will help you experience the relationship between control and relaxation. For some people, that experiment is enough; there's certainly no harm in trying it.

If that experiment isn't enough, try this one: Stand balanced on one leg. If you stand on one leg long enough, even while no joint visibly moves, you'll notice muscles in your body constantly and gently tensing and then releasing. You'll also notice that you don't know which muscles to tense and release; rather, this muscular response is nearly-instantaneous and impossible to consciously control. Your muscles simply react to what you *feel.*

From a technical perspective, balancing on one leg could not be simpler. Just stand there. But this is not to say that standing on one leg is easy, and it can be made even more difficult if there's excess tension, especially in the weight-bearing leg. Try it. As most knowledgeable yoga instructors will attest, excess tension makes balancing on one leg more difficult. The unnecessary tension tends to overcome the light muscular twitches that should occur. Either you'll lose your balance more quickly, or you'll compensate by using other areas of your body. You might, for example, start waving your arms, but, even then, you'll still probably lose balance faster than when you're relaxed.

Perhaps some yoga practitioners give attention to subtle muscular twitches when playing tennis, but few of the rest of us do. In total contrast, tennis players tend to focus on complicated tennis technique rather than on subtle muscular actions. With all of the complexity of tennis, it's not surprising that what we naturally neglect is what we can't easily see. When we focus on all those moving parts, we can easily forget that what's required for enhanced control in tennis is the same as what's required for better balance when standing on one leg. In both cases, excess tension interferes with making the subtle adjustments that you can *sense* but can't consciously control or explain. That is, both require subtle and subconsciously-derived muscular responses (tension and release) that only sufficient relaxation allows.

If relaxation enhances control by allowing the body to respond quickly to what it senses, then why do we tense up? We tense up for the sake of trying to control what cannot be consciously controlled. We struggle and strain, but, ironically, the extra effort actually detracts from our control. To control such subtle movements is beyond the conscious mind. As you repeat the experiment of standing on one leg, for example, notice again that the muscular twitches that you make could never be consciously controlled. Similarly, *it's impossible to consciously know exactly which muscles tense and release throughout a successful tennis motion*. Whether standing on one leg or hitting a tennis shot, any responses of tension and release will vary, with certainty, depending on what you *sense*.

Certain players are described as having exceptional control, often explained as "good touch" or "feel." Some believe these players simply have this "feel" or not, perhaps with the underlying assumption that it's an innate talent. Until you experience the boost of control provided by relaxation for yourself, you'll have to trust that the additional control can indeed be achieved.

To foster your trust, you might seek evidence and encouragement from high-performing athletes or musicians. Listen to how they talk, and, if you pay attention, they'll give you relevant clues. How relaxation is discussed might not be the same as it's presented in this book, but the underlying theme will be the same. You might hear them refer to "effortlessness" or "balance." As you understand by now from this book, effortlessness won't happen if some muscles are fighting against others. And balance is also a function of relaxation, and, in fact, often applied for the sake of better control.

When I've spoken with tennis professionals about relaxing the hands, they all know approximately what I am talking about. They do not, however, all talk about it in the same way that I do. For example, one former tennis touring professional told me that he does not relax his hands, but that he relaxes his wrists. *Puh-TAY-tow, Puh-TAH-tow…* The two ideas are essentially the same. I'm personally leery of talking about relaxing the wrists because it suggests excess movement in the wrists that I prefer not to encourage, but just try to fully relax your wrists without relaxing your hands. You can't — they're inter-connected.

I spoke with another former tennis touring professional after he had read an article of mine on the topic of relaxed hands, and he told me that the more power he's handling, the more he relaxes his hands. I was excited to hear this, and asked him how he conveys this concept to other people. To my dismay, he told me that he doesn't talk about it with anyone because it sounds too new-agey and not sufficiently technical.

People telling us about relaxation might use different language to describe it, or they might not talk about it at all. That doesn't mean it's not there. Keep trying. And when you experience it, you'll undoubtedly gain additional control.

4

MORE POWER

"The less effort, the faster and more powerful you will be."
–Bruce Lee

"I can control my passions and emotions if I can understand their nature."
–Baruch Spinoza

When boxers and other martial artists try to hit harder, they're often surprised by an ironic loss of power. The problem is excess tension, which causes some muscles to work against others. The relationship between power and tension also holds true for tennis, and probably for every sport.

If you were to tighten all of the muscles in your legs, for example, movement would become stiffer and more difficult. Running with such tension would be significantly slower and more tiring. The most extreme tensing of your legs would render them inflexible and immobile. Moving with excess tension is like driving a car in rush-hour traffic — minimally it slows you down, and at its worst it is like a traffic jam where you're stopped completely.

Perhaps you already possess plenty of power, but you can't control it sufficiently. In this case, if your ability to control your harder hit shots improved, then, for all practical purposes, you would gain power. In fact, as was presented in the previous chapter, relaxation can increase your control. The added control of relaxation applies to all shots, including stronger and faster shots. While all players have limits to the power they can reliably control, relaxation expands those limits.

If you try any relaxation drills from this book and find that you lose power as a result, then something's likely wrong with your technique. Diagnosing technical problems without seeing you play is not possible, but there are still some ideas that can help.

Power is achieved by accelerating the racquet head, so, for power, you must develop your ability to relax your hands and arms while simultaneously moving your racquet very quickly. This quick motion can be generated with body parts other than your hands and arms. Indeed, your legs and core can work together to create a quick motion that easily generates plenty of power.

Professional tennis players have leg and torso muscles that are primed for power, but most of them don't have big arms. They don't need big arms. Their arms and hands generally just go for the ride that their leg and core muscles create.

Your hands, through no particular effort of their own, can be very powerful at the end of a series of linked motions. Imagine the motion of a whip. The end of the whip is powerful yet "relaxed," having received its energy from a series of linked motions. Body parts passing energy from one to another is called the body's kinetic, or bio-kinetic, chain. (Important note: the word "whip" is not meant to encourage "whippy" or sloppy strokes; see Chapter 10 on Relaxation and Simplicity.)

Don't think you're too young or old for relaxing your hands and arms and subsequently unlocking greater power. You don't need to replicate the explosive, springing actions of the pros. With a simple and easy *sway* of your body, you can keep your hands and arms relaxed and generate more power than using your arm alone.

If you're steadfast in relaxing your hands and arms, then you'll likely discover your leg and core muscles engaging naturally. Your body will naturally find efficiencies that allow your shots to become more powerful.

If the previous paragraph seems startling to you, be assured that you read it correctly. To commit to relaxing your hands and arms has an effect on the rest of your body. In fact, there's a connection between relaxing your hands and arms for the sake of developing your technique, which will be explored farther in the next chapter, on Relaxation and Technique.

If you've tried relaxing your hands and arms and felt a loss of power, and your technique is adequately sound, then there's another possibility: you actually only *think* that relaxation caused you to lose power, whereas in fact you are as powerful as ever, or more.

That perceptions and reality aren't always the same probably isn't a shock to you. A corollary is that perceived exertions and real-life results don't necessarily correspond, as the following example makes clear. As part of a tennis drill, I once asked a student to tell me after each shot if his stroke was smooth or not. During the drill, the player hit a laser-like backhand that any pro would have admired. He also affirmed that the stroke had felt smooth. I assumed that he'd witnessed the connection between generating racquet head speed while remaining smooth until I heard him mutter, "But I didn't hit it that hard." I was astounded. I turned to his twin brother who was picking up balls nearby, and asked, "Did you just see that backhand? He blasted it, right?!" The brother confirmed what I'd seen: "Yeah, that ball was as hard as any shot he's hit in his life." The player felt smooth and in-control, and had crushed the shot, but because he lacked any sense of effort, his mind didn't register that he'd hit powerfully.

This mismatch between perception and reality is common. Many of us regard hitting powerfully as a strenuous exertion rather than as an application of technique and relaxation. As a result, we expect a sensation of effort in order to believe we're hitting powerfully. Releasing tension can cause tennis to feel *too easy*.

Before dismissing the possibility of this mismatch in your own mind, give some attention to your effort when you attempt powerful shots. Open yourself to the possibility of a shot feeling perfectly easy while also being powerful. You'll increasingly find that your most powerful shots feel very relaxed and effortless.

To be clear, tennis is an athletically-intense, whole-body sport that requires plenty of physical work. There's no contradiction, however, in also stating that hitting powerfully doesn't require much *sensation* of effort.

To improve, look for instances of extra effort having little effect, and, in contrast, of minimal effort having great effect. You may find that you've been focusing on the hands and arms aspect of tennis, and so applying extra effort to those parts of your body. Almost all of us instinctively have this perspective, and we should do our best to overcome it.

As a final note on effort, it is applied most effectively by engaging your legs. In fact, reducing excess tension in the hands and arms typically *requires* a simultaneous increase of movement in the legs. That is, minimizing what the arms do is made *possible* through efficient movement with the legs. When you provide sufficient support with your legs, then your arms and hands can just go for the ride, and you will have plenty of power. If leg movement is insufficient, however, then the arms must overcompensate. More on this in Chapter 10 on Relaxation and Simplicity

5

RELAXATION AND TECHNIQUE

"If you are going down a road and don't like what's in front of you, and look behind you and don't like what you see, get off the road. Create a new path!"
–Maya Angelou

"Invert, always invert."
–Carl Gustav Jacob Jacobi

There's a correlation between tennis technique and relaxation. In fact, if you've been applying what you read in other chapters, then you may have already experienced some improvement.

This improvement suggests that relaxation inherently leads to better technique. While this *can* be true, unfortunately, it's *not necessarily* true. If it were necessarily true, then many 4-year-olds would have amazing technique, and more adults might, like tennis-superstar Suzanne Lenglen, drink alcohol on court.

Does that make the converse notion true, which is that improved technique will lead to the relaxed efficiency that professionals so easily demonstrate? Does Federer's stellar technique *cause* his ability to play with such fluid motions? Again, no.

Technical flaws can *prevent* relaxation, and the removal of technical errors can *allow* relaxation, but great technique doesn't automatically *create* relaxation.

A player can have excellent technique and still strain like crazy.

More succinctly, there is simply a relationship between technique and relaxation, either for the better or for the worse. While poor technique can disrupt relaxation, excess tension can similarly disrupt good technique. Alternatively, the removal of technical imperfections can allow relaxation, and the removal of excess tension can in parallel allow for better technique.

Technique and relaxation should be combined productively. Sufficient technique *allows* relaxation and, in turn, relaxation *contributes* to better technique. This complementary feedback loop is true for every level of player from beginner to top professional.

If you haven't yet been able to hit with relaxed hands, then something's certainly wrong. What is wrong is not necessarily with your technique, but quite possibly it is. Until you can hit with relaxed hands, you will want to be especially wary of any technical problems, minimally for the sake of avoiding injury. Without my seeing you play, to diagnose any potential causes of injury is impossible, but just know that technical challenges are common. Every day I see poor technique creating limitations for players as to how much power they can handle or generate without excessive strain. Arm braces are rampant for the unfortunate reason that many stroking flaws lead to chronic tension, which in turn leads to chronic injuries.

Technical problems that could impede relaxation include poor body alignment, late preparation, incorrect ball contact point relative to the net, or reliance on the arms for power instead of coiling the body. (These topics will receive attention in more detail in Chapters 8, 9, and 10, on Stable Alignment, In Front, and Relaxation and Simplicity, respectively.)

Alternatively, to be able to keep your hands relaxed while hitting a stroke verifies that you did a long list of technical things correctly. In fact, you can always check some specific aspects of your technique with relaxation. As examples, if you're able to keep your hands relaxed throughout a stroke, then you know that you had an appropriate grip, met the ball with your arm and racquet in a stable alignment, prepared sufficiently early, and followed-through sufficiently. (See Chapter 8 on Stable Alignment, and Chapter 12 on the Follow-Through.)

To fail in any one of a number of aspects of technique will almost certainly cause strain and effort in your hands, and probably in other parts of your body as well. For the sake of challenging the interconnection between relaxed hands and good technique, allow yourself to prepare late for a ground stroke on purpose. Assuming the speed of the oncoming ball is at least slightly challenging, you'll find yourself largely unable to avoid excess tension. The fast and jerky change of momentum associated with late preparation *requires* excess tension.

If until now you believed that good technique would naturally lead to relaxed tennis and the graceful motions that professionals demonstrate, then you might be susceptible to a particularly troublesome pitfall, which is that good technique can also *hide tension*. In fact, hand and arm tension is particularly easy to hide.

This problem stems from a player learning what a stroke should *look like* to an outside observer. With enough practice, a player can achieve the *appearance* of a certain technique *without dropping excess tension*. If this is the case for you, then you'll have to find any excess tension for yourself. No one else can find it for you. Even coaches can be fooled by disguised tension because technique is generally assessed based on how it looks.

As an example, playing with excess hand tension often leads to an abbreviated follow-through. Coaches commonly respond to the shortened follow-through by showing a player how the follow-through should *look*. While a motion can be forced to appear technically correct, the original flaw of excess tension may remain intact. In other words, *the effect of the problem is addressed, but not its cause*. Many people inadvertently learn to hide tension this way. (See Chapter 12 on the Follow-Through.)

You might imagine that showing a player proper technique (such as the follow-through) is the only alternative. As a profoundly cataclysmic idea, what if I just skipped teaching some technique, like the follow-through? In fact, if the technique is just a natural by-product of being sufficiently relaxed, then the technique doesn't need to be taught at all. Instead, I can spend time more productively by helping my students understand the benefits of relaxation.

As it stands, there are a number of sub-topics in technique that I haven't taught for quite some time, including the follow-through. Many topics are just natural results of being sufficiently relaxed. You'll be relieved to know, however, that all of my students learn to follow-through properly. They discover that a follow-through is just information that indicates either sufficient, or insufficient, relaxation. Other than observing the follow-through in this respect, they spend no additional time on the topic.

On this point, certain topics of technique that are commonly taught and treated as important in fact don't need to be learned at all because they're by-products of relaxation. Giving those topics time and attention is actually a *waste of time*. Among my favorite moments as a teacher is discovering ways for someone to learn something without my having to "teach" it. You might similarly find enjoyment in discovering ways to simplify your thinking about tennis.

As you develop your understanding of relaxation, you'll begin to recognize some of these ways to simplify. That is, *understanding relaxation will help you distinguish between what's a technical fundamental, as opposed to what's a technical option, and/or by-product.* Some examples include what you should do with your wrist on any stroke, and which follow-through technique is best (see Chapters 11 and 12 on the Wrists and on the Follow-Through, respectively).

Not spending time learning topics that are inherent by-products of relaxation is both simplifying and liberating. In the classic book, *The Inner Game of Tennis*, author W. Timothy Gallwey promotes making things simpler for the conscious mind, and simultaneously leaving the subconscious mind to figure out the rest — which it generally does with a surprising amount of success. Correspondingly, the best tennis instructors often give less attention to adding things to your game, and more to removing extraneous obstacles in your path to improvement. *Not thinking about certain aspects of technique is a welcome removal of obstacles.*

Ultimately, the ability to relax the hands while hitting strokes is one of the best indicators of solid technique, and also one of the most valuable tools for working toward improvement. If a player perceives any significant tension in the hands while hitting any stroke, no matter how quickly the player is swinging, then something is wrong. Perhaps something is wrong with the stroke, or perhaps the stroke is fine but the player is too tense. Either way, it is only when the person relaxes sufficiently and uses good technique that the player's potential can be reached.

6

APPLYING AWARENESS

"For the things we have to learn before
we can do them, we learn by doing them."
–Hannah Arendt

"People wish to learn to swim and at the
same time to keep one foot on the ground."
–Marcel Proust

Awareness of tension is a skill that anyone can develop. In fact, you can demonstrate that you already have some of this skill by voluntarily flexing and releasing your hand.

Tennis tension constantly changes, and there is no single "right" tension to implement, but we can strive to understand some general limits. For example, consider hand tension for holding a racquet. One limit is the minimal amount required — the amount that keeps the racquet from leaving the hand during a stroke. In other words, don't let go of the racquet.

The other limit is too much tension, which is far more common. A quick way of knowing you've reached the limit of "too much" is if you feel any strain in your hand during a stroke.

Preferably, you'll hold on to the racquet very lightly. Regardless of the stroke, you should relax your hands as completely as possible, using only enough tension to avoid dropping your racquet. Ideally you will keep your hands feeling this relaxed throughout the entirety of any stroke. This is not to say there will be no tension, but rather the tension will be light and largely unnoticeable, with no sensation of strain.

You must experience relaxation before you can improve the skill. To help you learn to distinguish when you're adding excess tension, try the following awareness drill: Complete a forehand swing while gripping the racquet *tightly*. Notice how your swing feels. Repeat, and pay attention to how your arm, shoulder, hand and body feel throughout the swing. Remember the feeling.

Next, complete a forehand swing with *just enough* tension in your hand to maintain control of the racquet. Again, evaluate how that feels, and note how little tension you need to maintain control of the racquet. Finally, complete a forehand as you *normally* would and again evaluate how much tension you feel in your hand. Compared to the two outer limits that you first tried, is your normal forehand on the more-relaxed, or the more-tense side of the spectrum?

Repeat with the backhand. If you hit a two-handed stroke, you can try to evaluate both hands, but just paying attention to the dominant hand is simpler and probably sufficient. Andre Agassi said that, for a two-handed stroke, "you must relax at least one of the hands." And, ideally, both hands should be relaxed.

For the next drill, answer the following question after you hit each shot: "Was my hand relaxed?" If you feel no particular effort in your hand throughout the stroke, then after you hit the ball you'll say out loud, "Yes." (Ideally, you also avoid dropping the racquet!) If you squeeze your racquet handle enough to notice some strain during the stroke, however, then you'll say "No."

Of course, the desired rating is "Yes." This indicates no excess tension throughout the stroke. This shot will undoubtedly feel good. In fact, you'll want to hit this type of shot not only for the results, but also for the feeling of it. *Hitting a tennis ball should feel good.*

I highly recommend speaking every "Yes/No" rating out loud after you strike the ball, even if so quietly that no one else hears you. Saying the ratings out loud helps you maintain better focus and provides a gentle but constant reminder of what you're doing, whereas keeping the self-ratings in your mind enables you to more easily forget what you're doing. Keeping the ratings only in your mind is like focusing only on your breathing. You can do it, but usually not for long before your mind gets distracted. The mind typically likes to bounce around from topic to topic.

As a result of these drills, people often discover that they're squeezing far more than necessary, and sometimes even as hard as they can. Less sensation of effort is better than more, but any excess effort is still too much. *You do not want to feel any sensation of effort in your hands at all.* Easier said than done, of course, but that's the goal.

Lack of effort or strain may sound strange, but remember that you're just holding on to a tennis racquet, not lifting a heavy object. To hold onto a tennis racquet takes about as much effort from your hand as taking a standard book from a shelf. Again, this is not to say that there won't be any tension, but that the tension will be light and practically unnoticeable.

Try these drills with all of your strokes, including serves and net shots. The first step toward addressing excess tension in any shot is to know that the tension is there.

I also recommend trying these drills in practice prior to trying them during competitive situations. Give yourself the freedom to try the drills without concern for winning or losing. To feel what it is to play relaxed in the first place will likely be easier without the pressure of competitive urges.

I hope you'll give relaxation a fair chance. It might not lead to the best results immediately, so keep in mind that many positive changes can be temporarily disruptive. You must often get worse for a time before you can get better. You might also be pleasantly surprised by how much such awareness can help you improve. Once you start to feel how to play relaxed, and as you become more familiar with the feeling, you'll likely want to continue in large part *because of how good it feels*. As you enjoy the feeling of it, you'll also gain a trust in the worth of relaxation relative to your competitive results. Your competitive results will benefit from more control, probably more power, and better technique.

You can return to these drills regularly. Even when you know the feeling and value of relaxation, it's a challenge to maintain. Adjusting tension is one of the ongoing challenges in tennis for all of us. I personally feel as if I often *relearn* the value of relaxation. Excess tension seeps into my game, and only when I finally notice and remove it do I remember the value of being rid of it.

7

IMPROVING FASTER

"A man of genius makes no mistakes. His errors are volitional and are the portals of discovery."
–James Joyce

Relaxation can significantly increase the pace at which you improve. This mainly has to do with how you process information. Your tennis ability depends on information from outside your body, such as what is happening with the ball, and on information from your body itself, such as footwork and stroke movements. Relaxation helps you better apply that information for the best play in the moment, and additionally helps you collect and learn from new information for better play in the future.

As a model for this, imagine seeing your opponent hit a ball toward your side of the court. Your response to the oncoming ball is guided by the tennis experience you have accumulated up to now. Then upon hitting your shot, you observe the result in relation to what you intended. So while your response is derived from *previous* experience, your resultant shot also creates a *new* experience. This new experience links with your previous experiences, which are in turn cumulatively reapplied to your future play.

Through these actions, your improvement is guided by the new experiences that every shot creates.

These experiences provide an ongoing and evolving flow of information called a feedback loop. Repeating the loop helps you sort out which movements are best used (or not used) in various circumstances. As such, your likelihood to improve increases inevitably by hitting more shots.

Seemingly, playing more tennis alone should lead to a consistent and predictable rate of improvement. However, we all regularly (and frustratingly!) find ways to disrupt our feedback loops, thereby hindering our rates of improvement. If we're hitting more shots, how can we be hindering improvement? While the quantity of ball strikes indeed matters, quantity alone says nothing about the *quality*.

Fortunately, higher-quality information for our feedback loops is available via two different-yet-related methods: *tracking the ball,* and *relaxation*. Outside your body, you need high-quality information to accurately anticipate and recognize the timing and location of the oncoming ball. Inside your body, your specific *muscular movements* are similarly reliant on high-quality information. When you diminish the quality of these sources of information, you hinder your rate of improvement.

Of the ways to interfere with your sources of information, let's first consider tracking the ball. Tennis players have good reason to chide ourselves to "watch the ball." Coordinating movement to a ball and then successfully hitting it is an impressive feat in itself, but the challenge is made significantly easier with better information about where the ball is. (For additional information on improving your ability to track the ball, see Chapter 9 on In Front.) Conversely, not properly tracking the oncoming ball is inferior information and a common impediment to successfully hitting it.

Similarly crucial to the feedback loop, in order to assess the shot's success, is knowing where the ball goes *after* striking it. As for things that can go awry with your feedback loop, you will be encouraged to know that tennis players are typically quite good at collecting this particular information. Unfortunately, however, being anxious for information regarding a shot's success often causes players to look for the result before hitting the ball. Being too eager to know your result can interfere with your ability to achieve that result, so do your best to avoid looking for your result before you've struck the ball. Tracking the ball until you hit it provides the best information.

Now let's consider information inside your body. Gathering information from outside of your body allows you to use your experience to generate instructions for your body. These instructions materialize inside your body as *muscular tension and release*. That's where relaxation comes in. To best apply these instructions and move to the best of your ability, muscles should be relaxed. Relaxed muscles are *ready to receive and execute instructions* for how to tense and release.

In contrast, you can interfere with the application of information inside your body with excess tension. Tense muscles are too busy to receive instructions and unavailable for action because they are *already in use*. If you can't properly apply the experience/information you've collected, you'll likely play below your potential. Minimally, any excess tension impedes subtle muscular responsiveness, but, at the extreme, it can be debilitating — in fact, any completely tensed area of the body is effectively immobile.

When excess tension interferes with the execution of a shot, this also hinders what can be learned from that shot, thereby slowing overall improvement. You can't know the effect of instructions that weren't carried out, or that were carried out improperly. Any interpretation of the results for the sake of improvement would at best be muddled.

Excess tension further confuses the information in your feedback loop by creating an overabundance of information. If you made a successful shot, but did so with excess tension, understanding which muscles were useful will be more difficult. Excess muscular activity creates excess information to sort through, which can only reduce the efficiency of your feedback loop and further slow your improvement.

To be clear, to improve while playing with excess tension is still possible. With every struck tennis ball, you still generate a new experience with new information. What you can learn from the experience is simply diminished. The information for your feedback loop is jumbled. That said, there's a chance to benefit even from lower-quality information. A novice player, for example, usually benefits from almost any information regardless of its quality, as some information is generally better than none. As a player advances, however, higher-quality information becomes increasingly meaningful. While excess tension may not entirely prevent improvement, enhanced relaxation improves the efficiency of the feedback loop, enabling faster progress.

8

STABLE ALIGNMENT

"Let us permit nature to have her way.
She understands her business better than we do."
–Michel de Montaigne

Do you regularly suffer from tennis-related injuries? Do you consistently struggle with handling powerful shots, or with maintaining control when generating power? *Are you having trouble learning to relax for a particular stroke*? If the answer is "yes" to any of these questions, then you'll likely benefit from learning about "stable alignment."

Stable alignment is fundamental to good tennis technique, but (like relaxation) it's difficult to describe. The martial artists I know seem to understand stable alignment more readily than most other people. For the martial arts, whether generating power or handling power, your body should ideally be arranged so that it can *most easily* manage the forces placed on it. In other words, *some positions at once generate and withstand more force than others, with the same sense of effort.*

A tennis stroke similarly benefits in at least three ways from having a stable alignment: 1) a reduced-likelihood of injuries, 2) more efficiency in generating power, and 3) an increased ability to handle power coming from an opponent. The first benefit — reduced injuries — means your body is arranged to be optimally resilient against potentially injurious forces. While every athlete periodically gets injured during play, many injuries can be avoided with better (i.e., more stable) alignment.

Because stable alignment relieves your muscles of some work, such as the need for excess tension to protect you from injury, a fourth potential benefit can emerge, which is greater relaxation. In fact, a player *cannot consistently make a relaxed tennis stroke without stable alignment.*

Stable alignment has various requirements and options for each tennis stroke. In detail, the concept of stable alignment could be the subject of an entire book of its own, so what follows in this chapter is merely a fraction of the topic as a whole. I plan to provide additional resources (written and/or on-video) in the future, but, until then, perhaps this introduction will get you thinking about how the concept of stable alignment applied to your strokes can help you avoid injuries, handle and generate power more efficiently, and achieve greater overall relaxation.

For a simple example of body alignment making a difference, consider a one-joint movement, like the basic dumbbell biceps curl in weight-lifting. The curling movement is a simple bend at the elbow, but, for holding the weight, there are different options, such as with the palm facing up (which is standard) or palm facing down (i.e., a reverse curl). Neither palm-up nor palm-down is necessarily unstable, but most people can lift more weight with the palm-up version.

The difference between the palm positions is, of course, not due to the strength of the biceps changing, but instead due to other joints involved in the movement. In this comparison, the source of the difference is the *wrist*.

With the standard biceps curl, a weight that is challenging to lift would tend to press your palm *away* from the forearm at the wrist (i.e., wrist extension). This wrist position can generally accommodate more force with less risk of injury than some other positions. In fact, with a high degree of likelihood, you'd naturally put your wrist in this extended position to push against a heavy object.

For the reverse curl, however, a weight that is challenging to lift would press the palm *toward* the forearm at the wrist (i.e., wrist flexion), which, for most people, is a relatively weaker position. Generally, this position can handle far less force before it's at risk for injury. (Many martial artists strive to capture the wrists of their opponents in this weaker position.)

The wrist can move in other directions (radial deviation and ulnar deviation), but the point is not to discuss the wrist at length, but for you to understand that you would like your wrist to be in the most resilient and strong (stable) alignment possible for the sake of handling weight and avoiding injury.

Now consider a biceps curl as a part of a more complicated motion, again for which you could choose either palm-up or -down. If you're moving furniture, for example, you'd prefer the palm-up version if possible. This version is stronger in that it allows you to move heavier furniture, and more resilient in that it is less likely to cause an injury. Stable alignment increasingly matters as muscles get tired. If you move a lot of heavy furniture, to the point of significant fatigue, then stable alignment will increase in importance to you. By these parameters, you'd consider palm-up "more stable" than palm-down.

Likewise, stable alignment in tennis grows in importance as the game's physical requirements intensify. Conversely, unstable alignment impedes a player's ability to improve, restricting the ability to handle and generate power, or to fend off an injury.

Each major part of your body must be in a stable alignment for an overall stable tennis stroke. Certainly the wrist, forearm, elbow, and shoulder must all be arranged properly, but tennis involves the entire body, from the legs pressing against the ground to the angle of the wrist. Moreover, individual strokes have specific requirements for stable alignment, even for hitting different spins. For example, the continental grip is quite stable for hitting underspin on ground strokes or volleys, but generally isn't as stable for generating topspin.

The lack of a stable grip can even be a subtle source of injury. To use a grip that is not well-suited for the shot being attempted can lead to pain elsewhere. A common grip problem, for example, is hitting a one-handed backhand using a grip that's more suitable to the forehand side, requiring a suboptimal (unstable) wrist position to compensate. This strain on the wrist, ironically, can cause the common chronic injury called “tennis elbow” because that is where the pain is experienced. Indeed, sometimes a grip change is a simple and effective way to create a stable alignment for the wrist, which, in turn, is often a solution to elbow pain.

There is no “good” technique without stable alignment. Unfortunately, on every day that I see people playing tennis, which is nearly every day, I see poor body alignment that limits players’ potential to improve and that has caused or will cause injuries. Insufficient alignment is rampant. You might like to evaluate your own strokes for stable alignment.

For your evaluation, for every tennis stroke, it’s useful to imagine the body alignment with which you’d attempt the same stroke, but with a weight that’s *heavier* than a tennis racquet. As a start, you can even use a heavy, wooden tennis racquet to test your strokes. This isn’t a test of whether you’d play better with an old-style racquet, rather just a scan for excess strain uncovered by the additional weight. If some part of your body feels weak under the strain of a heavy racquet, it’s a likely point of failure for stability. And if that failure point can be adjusted and bolstered in some way for better resilience, such as with better technique, then there’s lower risk of injury, and a better chance of handling and generating power with ease.

Remember, relaxed hands are a great test for stable alignment and good technique (see Chapter 5 on Relaxation and Technique). If you can regularly make a stroke with relaxed hands, regardless of the oncoming ball's speed, then you likely have stable alignment for that stroke. If your hands reflexively tense up, however, then your technique probably needs an adjustment for more stable alignment.

9

IN FRONT

"It is impossible to speak in such a way that you cannot be misunderstood."

–Karl Popper

*"Watch the f****** ball!"*

–Anonymous

Like many other tennis players, you may have trouble tracking the ball sometimes. But you can improve this ability, and not just by concentrating harder. You can improve by hitting the ball farther "in front."

You may recall from Chapter 7, on Improving Faster, that tracking the ball and muscular tension are interrelated. Your mind calculates which muscles to tense and release for each stroke based on a range of information, and a significant part of that information is the ball's movement. Correspondingly, your potential relaxation is positively influenced by better tracking of the ball.

Though the foremost purpose of this chapter is to improve your ability to track a fast-moving tennis ball, as you read this chapter, you may notice ways in which concepts from Chapter 8, on Stable Alignment, are also interconnected.

"In front" basically refers to the direction to which you look to face your opponent. So, from the baseline of the court, the net and your opponent's side of the court are "in front" of you, and the baseline runs left-to-right next to you.

Hitting the ball "in front" entails reaching your arm(s) toward the oncoming ball so that the ball stays generally between your head and your opponent's side of the court. If the ball and your head are about equidistant from your opponent's side of the court when you strike the ball, then you're hitting the ball *next to you*. If your head is closer than the ball to your opponent's side of the court, then you're hitting the ball *behind you*. It's vastly preferable that the ball not get next to you, or behind you, prior to contact.

Tennis legend Chris Evert has said that among the best coaching tips she ever received was to "get behind the ball." For the record, there isn't much difference between "getting behind the ball" and hitting the ball "in front" other than the choice of words, just as the phrase "half of a dozen" also means "six." If you prefer thinking of "getting behind the ball" over hitting "in front," that is up to you — the result will be the same.

Evert said she applied this coaching tip to her ground strokes by imagining her torso as the vertex of a V, with her arms reaching forward as the extensions from the vertex. Watching Federer, Nadal, or Carlos Alcaraz hit ground strokes, you'll see them consistently reaching forward in this way. In fact, as they strike the ball, their arms are typically extended as far forward as possible. If you're unable to see how these great players meet the ball in front of them while they are in motion, then have a look at photos of them striking the ball. When the ball is on their strings, their arms are extended forward the vast majority of the time so that they can meet the ball in front.

Note that there isn't just one single contact point in front, nor do you need to fully extend your elbows like Federer, Nadal, and Alcaraz. In fact, there's a general range of contact points in front, with one end of the range being farther in front than another. If you extend your arm fully toward the net, it cannot be any farther in front. To bend your elbow(s) and/or move your arm(s) more toward a side can still be in front, though less so.

Tennis instruction manuals from over three decades ago advocated meeting the ball in front, although only just ahead of the front foot as you stepped forward into your stroke. This was still in front, but more to the side than how modern professionals typically hit the ball. Because modern equipment places greater emphasis on both handling and generating power, players' stances and grips have adapted to meeting the ball farther forward.

Meeting the ball farther in front may very well help you play better tennis, especially if you wish to compete against faster oncoming shots. Visual tracking of the ball becomes significantly easier by meeting the ball farther in front.

Picture a crowd of people watching a tennis match. People sitting at the sides of the court (near the net) get a neck workout, moving their heads back and forth to track the ball. But people sitting at the ends of the court (behind either baseline) barely move their heads. The ball is always in front of them — they don't need to move their heads in order to track the ball.

When you're playing rather than just watching, the ball's relative position to you similarly influences how you track the ball. If you keep the ball "in front" of you, you won't need to move your head much. If the ball gets more next to you, however, then you're more likely to turn your head quickly as you try to keep the ball within your sight.

Moving your head fast enough to maintain sight of the ball when it's traveling next to you is quite difficult (unless the ball's moving fairly slowly), and beyond certain speeds your head can't keep up as the ball travels from in front of you to next to you. If your head can't keep up, you'll lose sight of the ball. Instead, just keep the contact point in front, so you don't have to turn your head to maintain your tracking of the ball. You'll still occasionally be forced to hit the ball next to or behind you, but those contact points should be avoided unless you have no other choice.

High-speed photography and video show that most current professionals also move their heads slightly as the ball approaches, but these small movements are usually barely noticeable. A small amount of head motion is acceptable, but not much more. The classic tennis (and baseball, and golf, etc.) admonition to "keep your head still" remains generally relevant in the modern game.

Even touring professionals have limitations for seeing the ball when it's next to them. Notice photographs of pros hitting ground strokes and volleys, widely demonstrating contact points that are well in front, and the players' eyes are generally directed toward the oncoming ball. And alternatively, compare photographs showing ball-contact points next to the body, with the players' eyes often directed forward toward the opponent instead of on the ball. Ideally, we'd rather meet the ball in front with eyes directed toward the ball.

10

RELAXATION AND SIMPLICITY

"Perfection is finally attained not when there is no longer anything to add, but when there is no longer anything to take away."
–Antoine de Saint Exupéry

"Things alter for the worse spontaneously, if they be not altered for the better designedly."
–Francis Bacon

Have you played tennis in a relaxed way but felt your game was "loosey-goosey," unstructured, or undisciplined? Relaxation and technical simplicity may seem at odds, but you can indeed benefit from both simultaneously. You want to be relaxed, but not so much that your technique is sloppy. And you want your technique to be simple, but not with excess tension forcing the simplicity.

Relaxation and simplicity, in fact, can enhance one other. The merger of relaxation and simplicity is where you'll find your most efficient tennis, and, most likely, your best tennis.

Simple tennis strokes have minimal unnecessary movement, and less overall movement means less that can go wrong. Simple strokes improve the likelihood of timing a shot accurately, and are thereby more reliable.

Players commonly try “adding something” to their games, but few try to simplify. Both adding and subtracting have value in tennis, however, just like in mathematics and writing. Rather than just continuously adding components to your strokes then, also devote significant attention to removing the unnecessary. You will likely find simplification to be a surprising source of improvement.

If you’re an advanced player, you may consider yourself beyond thinking about simplification. *Nearly every tennis player, however, makes unnecessary motions,* and you can likely improve with simplification regardless of your current skill. Even the top pro players can benefit from simplification. For example, Venus Williams has a slight tendency to use excess motion for her forehand at her dominant shoulder joint when she strives for more power. Her forehand is also her ground stroke that is most likely to break down, which is no coincidence. Of course, her strokes are exceptionally successful in general, but, like the rest of us, any of the various links in her motions can make a difference.

As a personal example, for many years I imagined that my serve required more motion than it actually does for the pace I wanted. Ironically, by believing that I needed so much motion, I was holding myself back from the desired results. I could achieve sufficient pace, but the extra motion made timing more difficult. This reminds me of an observation by David Foster Wallace: “Any normal adult male can hit a tennis ball with a pro pace; the trick is being able to hit the ball both hard and accurately.”

Extra motion can be made in an infinite number of ways, so unfortunately it's not possible for me to assess your efficiency without seeing you play. Consider, however, that the most typical complication associated with relaxation is excess arm motion. In fact, excessive arm motion is the norm rather than the exception. We tend to initially interpret tennis as an "arm game," so nearly every tennis player is inclined to overuse the arm joints.

Again, advanced players aren't immune from this tendency. For example, I've observed countless advanced players with forehands that are over-complicated. One cause is that certain top professionals *appear* to make complicated motions, and amateur players try to imitate the motions without quite understanding what they see. Unfortunately, this often means that the wrong things get copied — by-products, flourishes, and idiosyncrasies — rather than useful fundamentals. Even some coaches are fooled by what they *think* they see some top professionals doing, and, in turn, promote complications in the games of their students.

Complicated forehands can be devastating to opponents, but can also break down mercilessly when pressured. I've noticed at least a few Division I college players having had such forehands. Their forehands were terrific — when they landed in — but they lacked consistency. In fact, one former player even struggled with the rudimentary drill of hitting forehands cross-court. He thought he needed more practice (and I suspect he also doubted his mental fortitude), but in reality he just needed simpler technique.

As a competitor, I check the strokes of my opponents for complications. In one instance, my opponent — the number 1 singles player for his college team — had a complicated forehand with exceptional topspin and power. At the beginning of the match, he hit enough clean winners to take three games in a row. His forehand was punishing against balls coming to him at "normal" pace. But when he faced more power to his forehand, his timing became unreliable. I noticed this, and consciously hit with more speed right into his forehand. My consistency didn't suffer much because I didn't try to hit near the lines; I just wanted to make him handle some power with his forehand. Initially, he seemed happy to hit what he considered his best shot. As the match went on, however, his forehand became a liability. By the end he was audibly questioning why he'd played so poorly.

Doing less with your arms frequently requires your legs to do more. As a corollary, when you use your legs sufficiently, your arms don't have to do as much. While we tend to regard tennis as an arm game, emphasizing it as a leg game can significantly boost your progress.

Of course, you already have some sense of the value of good footwork — you have to move to the ball. Furthermore, your legs get you into positions that enable how you *prefer* to use your arms to meet the ball.

Perhaps you prefer a forehand instead of a backhand, or a lower ball rather than a higher ball.

What's less obvious is the value of using your legs to *minimize what the arms must do*. The legs aren't just the key to what the arms *can* do; they're crucial for what the arms *don't have to do*.

For example, consider the classic tennis instruction, "swing the racquet, not the arm." This encourages players to move the racquet through the air, *not* by activating the arm joints, but by employing the legs and the torso. *When the legs and torso move, the arms will move as well*, even if the arm joints themselves do nothing.

Another classic tennis instruction for volleys is "fast feet and slow hands." In this case, the legs create forward momentum by stepping into the shot as it's struck. The arms simply go along for the ride that the legs provide.

To imitate the best professional strokes can be fun and instructive, but, let me caution you: because our minds like to look for motion, when we watch the top professionals, we tend to ignore what is *not* moving. When we see the top pros move their arms, those movements tend to be just individual quirks and inconsequential habits. By imitating these movements, we emphasize *optional* stroke components rather than simple fundamentals.

I intend to share more detailed analyses of touring professionals' strokes in future publications, but for now just keep in mind that the strokes of all top pros are much more similar than different throughout the essential portions of their strokes, and that these similar movements are also simple. Their strokes may not always *appear* very similar or simple, and each has recognizable flourishes and idiosyncrasies, but, rest assured, *each one has simple strokes where simplicity matters*.

Simplicity matters during the time the ball is struck and in the few moments prior. Before those moments, you can do all sorts of wild things and those things won't matter. And after you've struck the ball you can do even more crazy things since the ball is already gone. If you keep your tennis technique sufficiently simple in those brief moments leading up to and through striking the ball, however, then you're likely on the right track.

As another reminder, consider your hand tension. Your hand only needs to squeeze enough to keep the racquet from leaving your hand. There's nothing particularly complicated about that. So, if you feel you're moving your legs sufficiently, but are still noticing hand and/or arm tension, then your technique might need attention (see Chapter 5 on Relaxation and Technique, and Chapter 8 on Stable Alignment).

11

THE WRISTS

"Truth is ever to be found in simplicity,
and not in the multiplicity and confusion of things."
–Isaac Newton

"Freedom is nothing but a chance to be better."
–Albert Camus

How much should your dominant wrist move during a tennis stroke? Top professionals make some wrist movements, but how much? *Too much* makes timing, and thereby control, exceedingly difficult, while *too little* inevitably introduces unnecessary tension. The subtle answer lies in the relationship between relaxation and simplicity (see the previous chapter). What you want is: *no strain to prevent the wrist from moving, yet no deliberate effort to direct the wrist to move.*

To remove extra effort from the hands and arms largely enables this optimal balance of relaxation and simplification at the wrist (assuming your general technique is reasonably sound; see the next page). The wrist is not moved intentionally, but is instead moved in response to the movement of larger and more active parts of your body — the wrist is carried on a ride, of sorts. This is the wrist movement we see in the play of top professionals.

The ideal amount of wrist movement is quite delicate. If you *feel* muscles at work to move your wrist, such effort is probably too much. And yet, if there's noticeable effort to *prevent* movement, then that's also too much. The limitation of movement should be as natural and effortless as the movement itself.

Some technical requirements must be met in order for your wrist to function as it should. At a minimum, for every stroke you will need an appropriate grip and stable wrist alignment (see Chapter 8 on Stable Alignment). And if you can't make a stroke without effort at the wrist, then something is wrong. If the problem is with your technique, you'll want to give this immediate attention (see Chapter 5 on Relaxation and Technique). Excess wrist strain typically leads to injuries.

With proper fundamentals in place, no additional time needs to be spent thinking about what the wrist should or shouldn't do. For a forehand, for example, as your legs and torso pull your arm and racquet forward, your wrist should naturally drop back, or drag, into extension. To prevent this natural action would require excess effort. As the stroke continues forward, your racquet will pull slightly but constantly at your wrist, causing your wrist to move subtly through the swing. This amount of wrist movement is natural and optimal.

The same applies for your wrist to your other strokes. Proper volleys, for example, generally involve a compact motion, so the weight of your racquet won't pull at your wrist as much as during a ground stroke. As a result, for a volley your wrist will naturally move much less, and perhaps not at all.

For your serve, you should neither strain to prevent wrist movement nor try to move your wrist. Again, the weight of the racquet naturally pulls your wrist, unless you apply tension to direct or prevent it.

What a boon to liberate our minds from any concerns about how the wrist should or shouldn't move. This simplification allows us to *redirect our focus* to critical fundamentals. In fact, much of technique emanates from the synergistic association of simplification and relaxation. Examining tennis through this lens leads to the realization that many aspects of technique don't need to be proactively learned (see Chapter 5 on Relaxation and Technique). What a time saver.

Of course, there's nothing *wrong* with learning every possible detail in tennis technique, especially if it's interesting and enjoyable, regardless of its value to actual success on the court. For the serve, knock yourself out learning technical specifics like wrist extension, radial deviation, and forearm supination, followed by wrist flexion, ulnar deviation, and forearm pronation. As you learn these details, however, you'll also benefit from the perspectives of relaxation and simplicity. In the context of relaxation and simplicity, *the details become less mysterious*. As long as other components of a stroke are technically sound, *simply make sure you don't apply effort that in any way modifies your wrist's natural movement.* You can let your wrist and forearm go for the ride that the pull of the racquet provides.

12

THE FOLLOW-THROUGH

"In order to go on living one must try to escape the death involved in perfectionism."
–Hannah Arendt

"It is not your paintings I like, it is your painting."
–Albert Camus

"So simplify the problems of life, distinguish the necessary and the real."
–Henry David Thoreau

Does a tennis stroke's follow-through matter? In some sense, no. Imagine two strokes that are identical through contact with the ball, but one stroke continues its motion after striking the ball, whereas the other stroke is abruptly truncated following the strike. Theoretically, the results of the two strokes remain the same, because once the ball leaves the strings, whether the follow-through then happens or not is irrelevant. By the time the follow-through either transpires or doesn't, the ball's trajectory has already been determined.

The follow-through is distinctly relevant, however, in its *relationship with tension.* Stopping or manipulating a follow-through requires unnecessary muscular tension, for which there's no added benefit. To make an effort and receive no benefit is a waste of energy, and therefore *inefficient*.

Alternatively, to allow a stroke to decelerate in its own time entails *no significant extra effort*, so following-through is just an *efficient* extension of working fundamentals. This lack of effort correspondingly contributes to control and power, and reduces fatigue and risks for injury.

Most of us can accurately assess whether a follow-through looks wrong. If it appears awkward, it typically is. But does a good-*looking* follow-through necessarily demonstrate sufficient relaxation? Unfortunately, not always. In fact, a follow-through can be made to look good while at the same time disguising excess tension. And excess tension, hidden or not, still limits one's tennis potential.

Recall from Chapter 5 that technique and relaxation are interconnected, and that good technique *allows* for relaxation, but does not necessarily *create* relaxation. Also recall that technique can hide tension. As a corollary, following-through in a manner that looks right doesn't always remove underlying tension, much like pain medication only treats pain, not the underlying injury. The effect is treated, but not the cause.

Hidden tension can be even more problematic than overt tension. Players who inadvertently bury tension often feel confused and frustrated. They follow-through as instructed, and often look good on video, but their results tend to remain below expectations. Many start to doubt their mental strength, though their actual shortcoming is their obliviousness to obscured excess tension. If only these players could understand the connection between relaxation and technique, then they would not be driven to question their mental fortitude.

With proper fundamentals in place, a fine follow-through is actually difficult to stop, and generally requires excess effort/tension to stop it. For practical purposes, the follow-through is a by-product of secure fundamentals; it's an indicator. Thus, it ideally emerges on its own and looks correct naturally. Therefore, if a follow-through doesn't look or feel right, resist the urge to manipulate it. Instead, scrutinize the stroke that leads up to it. Whatever flaws exist in a stroke, the follow-through is never the source of those problems. At best, the follow-through may gauge whether a stroke has gone well or poorly. Deeming the follow-through itself as problematic focuses on the effect of a shortcoming, not the cause. As a consequence, a skilled coach can typically correct a follow-through solely with attention to the prior components of the swing.

You may find variations of following-through interesting, but you shouldn't try for a particular type. Instead, just observe what you do naturally. Again assuming you have solid fundamentals, any number of follow-through styles can be acceptable. Your follow-through may already resemble that of some highly-successful and famous tennis pro, depending on factors like the type and amount of spin you generate, the weight and balance of your racquet, and other variables.

My follow-throughs, for example, tend to vary most depending on the weight and balance of the racquet that I'm using.

If you're hung up on your follow-through, attention to hand and arm tension will likely help diagnose and resolve the underlying cause. At the very least, notice how tightly you grip your racquet, and you'll likely notice the relationship between hand tension and the follow-through. Be forewarned, however, that finding the optimal tension is rarely as quick as we hope it will be.

For quicker progress, you may be tempted to implement a mechanical version of the follow-through. And instruction that promises a fast solution in this way exists in abundance. The bulk of these solutions are derived from examples of professional players who we're encouraged to mimic, with the implication that if it's good enough for them, then it will work for you too. While there's nothing wrong with quick progress, be wary of quick fixes that potentially hinder your long-term development. What a famous player does may or may not be right for you. To mimic a particular follow-through disregards individual styles and special circumstances; stringent imitation simply won't accommodate all possible variables. In fact, different great players follow-through differently from one another, and even the same player will follow-through in a variety of ways depending on the situation. More importantly, imitating a pro doesn't prevent disguising tension (see Chapter 5 on Relaxation and Technique) — and, in fact, often promotes it. A good follow-through isn't developed by manipulating your muscles to re-create the style of someone else. A good follow-through is to use good technique through contact with the ball, to relax, and to see what you naturally do.

If your follow-through for a particular stroke does not look like the famous player that you would like to imitate, take consolation from the fact that there is no standard follow-through for great players. For example, the forehands of Federer, Nadal, and Novak Djokovic all tend to finish differently.

For us to give attention to the interdependence between the follow-through and relaxation helps us understand why we follow-through. We don't follow-through just because it looks right or because some great player does it. Rather, we follow-through for the same reasons a great player does: we follow-through to avoid the pointless and inefficient effort that would go with stopping a follow-through. Why make an effort for no benefit when making a proper follow-through is effortless?

13

THE RACQUET

"The world of reality has its limits;
the world of imagination is boundless."
–Jean-Jacques Rousseau

If you've assiduously heeded the advice so far in this book but still consistently struggle to keep your hands and arms relaxed, the reason may involve your racquet. Relaxation requires that your racquet be *sufficiently stable for the power you want to handle*. The faster the oncoming ball, the more stable your racquet must be in order to minimize the jolt of impact. A racquet that's insufficiently stable for the power you're confronting isn't conducive to relaxed hands and arms, and, more importantly creates greater risk for arm injuries.

For ample stability, you'll need to evaluate grip size, grip shape, head size, overall weight, and weight distribution. There's plenty of good advice on these topics outside of this book.

Despite all of the good advice available, people make mistakes. The most frequent mistake is selecting a racquet that's *too light for the level of competition*. Warren Bosworth, the renowned racquet technician, once told me that touring professionals must use a minimum racquet weight in order to be *consistently* competitive. His observation might naturally lead you to consider your own racquet's weight in relation to your level of competition.

Though there's no exact formula that specifies racquet weights for different players, long-standing advice dictates choosing the heaviest racquet that's tolerable. The reasoning for the advice stems from what is most easily known: While almost everyone knows when a racquet is too heavy, usually only experienced players realize when a racquet is too light. With this in mind, your best chance to choose a racquet that is neither too heavy nor too light is to select a racquet that's only slightly lighter than your upper-limit of tolerable weight.

The stability of your racquet matters for the sake of relaxed hands and arms, but is even more important for the sake of injury prevention. One reason players gravitate to lighter racquets is chronic arm injuries. They assume less weight is easier on the arm. Yet surprisingly, one possible solution for arm pain is using a *heavier* racquet. (Really!) *Between two racquets that are identical in every respect except weight, the heavier racquet is likely more helpful in reducing tension and strain.* While good technique is the best defense against arm injuries, even players with good technique can suffer from arm problems as a result of playing with a too-light racquet.

I learned the value of a heavier racquet the hard way. I briefly switched to a racquet that was about 30 grams lighter than is typical for me, drawn by the usual attractions: more maneuverability, and a *sensation* of more power. (In reality, my shots weren't necessarily more powerful, but they *seemed* more powerful because, whenever I had time to swing, I felt able to swing slightly faster.) While playing with a lighter racquet is fine for generating power, a player must also *handle power*. Tennis balls only weigh about 2 ounces (~57 grams), but a fast-moving ball can still make quite an impact. A heavier racquet protects the arm better against the shock of a fast-moving ball, whereas a lighter racquet is more easily jarred and twisted by oncoming shots. In this way a heavier racquet is *more stable*. Imagine a tennis ball hitting a piece of paper versus hitting a brick. Granted, neither weight is comparable to that of a tennis racquet, but the comparison nevertheless illuminates the point that greater weight gets jolted less. In my case, the loss of stability associated with lower racquet weight caused me to brace and tense my hands and arms reflexively, eventually causing pain in my arm. After switching back to a heavier racquet, I had to re-learn that the heavier racquet would protect my arm before I could stop reflexively bracing against powerful shots. Once I dropped the tension, the pain soon disappeared.

Some players assume that using a heavy racquet causes arm injuries just by having to move the extra weight through the air. We're not talking about power weight lifting, however; the heaviest racquets currently available weigh less than 13 ounces (~368 grams). Most people don't endure much strain to move such little weight. Granted, a heavy racquet may grow tiresome to wield, but fatigue isn't an injury. Children often begin learning tennis with old heavy racquets found in their garages and basements. They might play better with lighter racquets, but at least the heavier weight generally isn't a risk for arm injuries. In fact, the opposite is true. Lighter racquets are more conducive to arm injuries.

Another benefit of using a heavier racquet is needing to swing *less quickly* to generate *the same power*. One of my former students who played Division I college tennis observed, "You can swing faster with lighter racquets, but, to generate the same amount of power, you *must* swing faster." (Well said, Trevor.) Admittedly, swinging faster can be fun, but it's not always better for competitive results. A heavier racquet borrows power from the oncoming ball more readily. (And not having to swing as quickly to generate the same power *makes timing easier*.)

Generally, players are able to manage heavier racquets as their technique improves. Rather than waiting for your skill to improve sufficiently to try a heavier racquet, however, consider "playing up" to a heavier racquet now. Your play may suffer initially, but over time you'll likely adjust to the added weight with better technique. Using a heavier racquet can, in fact, provide a good checkup for your technique. If you're using good technique, the effort to move the racquet through the air comes mostly from your legs and torso, not from your arm (see Chapter 10 on Relaxation and Simplicity). Even the heaviest racquets should feel easily manageable by your relatively strong torso and legs. If your current technique involves significant effort from your arm, however, a heavier racquet will feel more unwieldy. (And, of course, using lots of arm effort is the opposite of what this book encourages.)

Finding a racquet that's sufficiently stable relative to the pace of oncoming balls isn't always easy. Even top players make adjustments. (And most pros have their racquets customized to be heavier than what is available for retail sales.)

To experiment with a heavier racquet, consider temporarily customizing a racquet you already own, using lead or tungsten tape. By using weighted tape you will learn with your own racquet how added weight can influence a racquet's performance. The placement of the extra weight can affect your racquet's balance, sweet spot location, stability, and power. For more information on the topic, you will find countless online tutorials.

While this chapter generally encourages you to consider the benefits of a heavier racquet, no specific weights are endorsed because there is no one right answer. Your playing style, skill level, *desired* skill level, and tendencies for injury all impact the proper weight for you. Experiment to find the optimal weight range for you, and continue to ponder the classic tennis tip of using the heaviest racquet you can bear.

14

APPLICATION EXAMPLE: VOLLEYS

"We know not through our intellect
but through our experience."
–Maurice Merleau-Ponty

"A design isn't finished until someone is using it."
–Frank Lloyd Wright

Every tennis shot, like each snowflake, is unique. The trajectory, spin, and speed of each oncoming ball always varies at least slightly, and your reactions must vary in kind. To respond successfully and consistently requires subtle muscular adjustments that only sufficient relaxation allows. Alternatively, the rigidity and inflexibility of excess tension negatively affects your ability to make subtle adjustments.

Players who volley well constantly alter the tension in their hands and arms for control. They're commonly lauded for having good "feel," "touch," or "hands." If you practice volleying with sufficiently relaxed hands and arms, you'll develop control and "feel" with your volleys as well. (And again, your rate of improvement relies upon how relaxed you are; see Chapter 7 on Improving Faster.)

No useful level of hand and arm tension includes the sensation of strain, yet one cause of excess tension in the hands and arms during volleys is believing it's necessary. Perhaps a coach even encouraged this belief with common volley instructions like "firm your hand," "firm your wrist," or "squeeze the racquet." Words such as "firm" and "squeeze" may help novice players to some degree, but such cues lack sufficient clarity and are easily taken too far. Many players misconstrue such cues to mean squeezing as hard as possible. Instead, what is desirable is to learn to volley with hand and arm tension that *varies* according to the circumstances of play.

Any tension-related misunderstandings tend to be heightened because a firmer hand is, in fact, associated with more power. Keep in mind, however, that your most powerful volleys can still be produced by a relaxed and light-feeling hand and arm. Though this may seem contradictory, to be *sufficiently firm for a powerful volley requires no sensation of effort or strain.*

Consider performing a weight lifting exercise such as a standard biceps curl. If I do the exercise with an ink pen in my hand, my muscles move with some light effort, but there isn't a palpable sensation of exertion. Even quadrupling the weight to four ink pens feels about the same. There's undoubtedly a limit to how many ink pens I can curl without strain (if I could hold that many), but the point is I can adjust what's required without noticing any particular strain.

Now imagine rating your experience of hand and arm tension for a volley on a scale of 0 to 10, with noticeable strain beginning at 7, and with 10 being squeezing as hard as you can. With little or no change in technique from one volley and another other than varying your hand tension alone, you can generate a wide range of results, roughly in accordance to your tension self-ratings. For example, a soft touch shot like a drop volley requires very light tension and a low rating, say from 1 to 3. Alternatively, to drive the volley by borrowing power from the oncoming ball, hand tension moves to a higher range, perhaps from 4 to 6. And while you will vary your ratings with different sorts of volleys so that less tension is associated with reducing power and more tension with increasing power, a *feeling of strain or effort indicates too much tension.* Yes, a lower rating such as a 1 is going to give you a different result than a higher rating such as a 6, but, crucially, you never want to go to 7 or beyond. *The consistently useful range of tension involves no sensation of effort or strain.*

While finding the right tension is a challenge, at least we can avoid the amount of tension that is clearly wrong, which is the amount at which we feel effort and strain. Any sensation of effort or strain will cause a loss of feel and control, and, if repeated, fatigue, or worse, injury.

Some highly-skilled net players I know have remarked that they try to squeeze the racquet handle at the moment the ball hits their strings, and "squeezing" might seem like a contradiction of the value of relaxation for volleys. To associate the momentary squeeze with tension leaves out a crucial detail, however, which is that a hand squeeze must be preceded by lower hand tension. Moreover, the majority of subtle adjustments in tension for successful net play are completed prior to ball contact. So as long as there's sufficient relaxation during preparation, *the squeeze-at-contact is largely irrelevant.*

For a player to benefit from any relaxation that precedes a squeeze might be an improvement, so I'm not strictly opposed to squeezing-at-contact for volleys, but I'm not that eager to promote the idea either. A player who is no longer dependent on that cue has freed up some mental space.

We tend to lightly squeeze at contact whether or not we try, just to keep the racquet from twisting on off-center hits. This hand twitch should remain barely perceptible. If you regularly notice more than a subtle twitch, then something's wrong, and excess tension is holding you back from achieving your volleying potential.

Awareness of a problem is always the first step in finding a solution (see Chapter 2 on Awareness of Tension). After detecting excess tension, the next step becomes getting a proper diagnosis of the source of the excess tension, as there are multiple potential causes.

Poor volleying technique is a rampant cause of excess hand tension (and of chronic injuries, such as tennis elbow). Technical requirements include certain grips and arm positions that allow meeting the ball stably (see Chapter 8 on Stable Alignment). Modern professional tennis players typically use the Continental grip for both forehand and backhand volleys, but there are acceptable variations. Meeting the ball in a stable position generally coincides with meeting the ball in front, helping to track the ball (see Chapter 9 on In Front). And, of course, volleying well generally requires the use of your legs to minimize what your arms must do (see Chapter 10 on Relaxation and Simplicity). If you can relax your hands while hitting forehand and backhand volleys in practice, then, with few exceptions, you have some verification that you did a long list of things correctly (see Chapter 5 on Relaxation and Technique).

Technique is of great importance, but you can hit with great technique and still miss badly due to extra tension that stems from competitive pressure. Many players feel a great deal of stress specifically when approaching the net. Awareness can again help you address the tension. Recognizing excess tension enables you to modify your play, perhaps by aiming for easier targets (see Chapter 15 on Competing in Relation to Tension). Staying relaxed isn't easy during stressful competitive scenarios, but, if you give regular attention to the challenge, the ability can be improved.

Here's a practice drill for changing tension in your hands to alter volleys. One player, the feeder, hits balls from the baseline to another player standing near the opposite side of the net, the volleyer. The volleyer has two potential targets: one deep in the opponent's part of the court, and one close to the net in the opponent's part of the court. As the feeder hits each ball to the volleyer, the feeder calls out to which of the two targets the volleyer should aim, either "deep," or "short." With very little motion, the volleyer then attempts to place the ball according to the feeder's instruction. This drill offers chances for the net player to make quick decisions, to use very little motion in favor of timing and disguise, and, of course, to feel the correct amount of hand tension required for the different shots. Ideally, you as the volleyer will notice that hand tension alone can change your results.

15

COMPETING IN RELATION TO TENSION

*"It's one on-one-out there, man.
There ain't no hiding. I can't pass the ball."*
–Pete Sampras

Players commonly feel as if they play better in practice than in competition.* The difference between the two situations is often the tension associated with each. This book is not specifically about handling excess tension that stems from competition, but because competing has a natural tendency to hinder relaxation, the relationship deserves some attention.

Before the topic of competition-related tension is addressed, first ask yourself if you follow the common practice of ignoring the subject when competition is not immediate. If so, be clear that *relaxation is a constant fundamental goal* regardless of what might disrupt it

---

*This feeling can be perpetuated by the lack of an objective measure of "playing well." When practicing, players often ignore mistakes, whereas when competing, the assessment typically shifts to the match score. Without objective measures to apply equally to practice and competition, we're free to create inaccurate narratives about how we're playing (most often "better" in practice, "worse" in competition). In the absence of unbiased evaluation, people commonly *overestimate* their abilities in a variety of realms (such as car-driving, music, logic, and humor). To learn more about this cognitive bias, research the Dunning-Kruger Effect.

(see Chapter 16 on the Habit of Relaxation). Similarly, you shouldn't just track the ball ("watch the ball") when there is competitive pressure, but instead you should track the ball whether you are competing or not.

A simple solution to competitive tension is to stop competing, and most players benefit from this occasionally. Competing, though, has some constructive benefits, including learning to deal with tension more effectively. Tension is a lifelong challenge for nearly everyone, and one reason to play tennis is to develop tension-handling skills.

Players who respond well to tension are often said to compete well, and for this there are two effective approaches. The first is reducing or eliminating excess tension. Serena Williams highlighted this skill in relation to her competitive results in a Sports Illustrated interview in 2015: "I've won most of my matches, probably all of my grand slams, because of what's upstairs, not anything else." She went on to emphasize the importance of relaxation when it's most needed: "If you're behind in a game, it's so important to relax, and that's what I do. When I'm behind in a game, that's when I become most relaxed."

For the sake of playing to your potential, the pursuit of tension-reducing skill merits persistent attention. In fact, to improve in this way might be the essence of the lifelong challenge of tennis for you and every player. The closer you can get to an optimal level of tension during play, the better. When you achieve the right tension, you can play to your potential. Enjoy those golden moments.

No one can stay free of excess tension all the time, which is why we need a second approach to competing well. The second approach is managing your play with respect to your current level of tension.

To understand this approach, first consider that competition regularly requires decisions based on a range of variables. How you choose to play may be influenced by the score, your playing style in relation to that of your opponent, injuries, the weather, your fitness and that of your opponent, the round of the tournament, and so forth.

Tension informs competitive decisions as much as any other factor. And because tension inherently varies, it is an ongoing source of information. That is, how you play should fluctuate from moment to moment in accordance with your ever-changing level of tension, even during individual points. In the same way that you adjust your play to shifting winds or light, you should adjust your play to tension.

While excess tension interferes with your ability to play with maximum control and power, and can therefore keep you from reaching your highest playing potential, competing well does not necessarily require playing well.

To compete well, regularly assess your current tension and correlate it with your range of competitive choices. With your current level of tension, what shots should you choose? There is no right answer to this question — your skills and other variables will inform such decisions — but, good news, you can improve at adjusting to your tension like you would improve any other skill.

While there is no correct answer to how you should adjust your play to tension, responding well to excess tension generally entails adjusting appropriately with regard to risk. That is, when you are experiencing greater tension, you should be more selective with your risk-taking. To reduce risk, you can choose to hit your most reliable shots, and/or add margins of safety. Examples of adding margins of safety include aiming comfortably farther from any lines, and/or aiming for higher net clearance, and/or adjusting the type or amount of spin, depending on what gives you more confidence.

So for the moments when you cannot adjust your tension to how you want to play, try adjusting how you play to your tension. Doing so can help you find your range and build some rhythm and confidence. This, in turn, might be just what you need to adjust your tension and thereby reach your playing potential.

16

THE HABIT OF RELAXATION

"We are what we repeatedly do.
Excellence, then, is not an act, but a habit."
–Aristotle

If you've begun applying relaxation to your tennis from reading this book, you may have already had moments of spectacular play and leaps of considerable improvement. You may also have discovered that you can't always sustain it, especially when you want to play your best (see Chapter 15 on Competing in Relation to Tension). Unfortunately, maintaining the right tension can't be perfected. In fact, as John McEnroe commented, "Everybody chokes." On a more positive note, however, you can continue to improve your relaxation skills. The first step is the realization that relaxation affects your ability to play well, and the next step is heightening your awareness of tension. This requires more than a one-time effort; it's a perpetual challenge. To improve your consistency with relaxation, engage in the challenge as often as is practical. Checking tension regularly can become a pleasant habit, and with it you can expect steady improvement.

In fact, checking tension can habitually occur *before every single point* as a part of a pre-serve or pre-return ritual. You might already have a pre-point ritual, as does every tennis professional. Rituals vary widely and can include almost anything, limited only by time-related rules, social conventions, and your imagination. Players commonly make rituals of twirling or flipping their racquets, bouncing a ball, tapping their shoes, tugging at their clothes, making hand movements, toweling off, and tying their shoes. Nadal is regularly at risk for a time violation because of his extensive pre-point ritual.

Most successful players understand that pre-point rituals are an aid to relaxation, but what most players don't know, ironically, is that a *part of that ritual can specifically include checking for sufficient relaxation and/or adjusting tension.* For example, part of your ritual can be specifically checking hand and arm tension before every point and adjusting appropriately. A former student of mine made relaxing her hand a visible part of her ritual by dangling her hand in a relaxed way prior to every point. This gesture was one piece of a complex but short ritual that helped her progress to two high school state singles finals.

What follows may sound basic and obvious, but it must be said: *In order to garner the benefits of what's suggested in this book, you must practice the skill of relaxation with consistency*. Reinforce relaxation like you would technique, strategy, fitness, or any other element of the game.

Like all skills, relaxation can be improved but never perfected. The chance to refine the skill is one more reason why tennis is a sport for a lifetime. Practice relaxation like you'd practice a serve, backhand, or any other tennis skill.

You would also like to practice the skill of relaxation *independently of competitive play*. Inattention to relaxation when you're "only" practicing, with the expectation of conjuring it as needed in matches, is a mistake. Relaxation certainly feels easier when you're "only" practicing, and correspondingly may then seem less important, but developing the *habit* of attention to relaxation is what truly requires diligent practice. You must routinely implement the skill to maintain it.

With diligent practice, you'll gain trust in your ability to relax. With this trust, you'll build *confidence*, which in turn will allow you to play to your potential. Your playing potential is not defined by your best shots, but rather it is limited by what you can do under pressure. Perhaps the saying "You're only as good as your second serve" should be amended to: "You're only as good as the shots you can hit under pressure." All top players can reliably hit their shots in a relaxed way while under intense pressure.

Recall from Chapter 2 on Awareness of Tension that there's no practical distinction between types of tension so that, for example, mental tension will affect your physical ability. One type of tension can't exist without the other, at least for any significant length of time. Mental tension is perhaps not exactly the same as physical tension, but the interconnection is significant enough that they can be addressed simultaneously. In which case, you might find it easiest to pick one physical area to relax, and practice relaxing that area. The primary suggestion in this book has been the hands.

While awareness of hand tension doesn't guarantee instant mastery of overall tension, it provides a starting point from which to progress, and it affects your tennis ability. The "drill" for evaluating hand tension, or any specific body part, is straightforward. Simply ask whether your hands feel tension, strain, or effort, or whether they instead feel easy, effortless, and relaxed. Regardless of how nuanced your sensitivity is, you should be able to distinguish this much. Asking this question prior to each point is a positive habit, and the answer provides crucial information for subtle adjustments that increase your odds of performing well.

You might like to try some off-court relaxation rituals for your non-tennis life as well. Off-court rituals will help develop the skill of relaxation more generally. This will also, of course, help you play better tennis.

Just like on-court rituals, off-court rituals can be anything, limited only by your imagination and social conventions. Generally, relaxation rituals involve the art of shut-up-and-release-tension-for-a-moment; common examples are meditation, yoga, making tea, and reading. We become what we do, and what we do is largely derived from habits. Making a habit of sensing and adjusting tension can positively affect your entire life.

17

FINAL THOUGHTS

"Guarding knowledge is not a good way to understand. Understanding means to throw away your knowledge."
–Thich Nhat Hanh

"The face is the soul of the body."
–Ludwig Wittgenstein

This book isn't meant to be encyclopedic, so for simplicity, I've intentionally *not* included many subtopics of relaxation. Some examples include breathing (and grunting!), the natural elements (because standing in the wind, let alone playing tennis in it, can trigger excess tension), and the interconnection between relaxed tennis and beauty/aesthetics. Perhaps most surprisingly skipped is an exploration of peak ("magical-feeling") psychological experiences. Excess tension significantly reduces the odds of feeling good when striking a ball, and consequently eliminates opportunities for peak experiences. So, while relaxation isn't the same as peak experiences, it's a mandatory ingredient.

Connections between tensions in different areas of the body might also be a worthy topic for exploration. For example, I read somewhere that if you relax your tongue completely, then you'll have relaxed all the excess tension in the rest of your body. Michael Jordan and Pete Sampras were cited as examples who were, in fact, famously photographed playing with their tongues hanging out of their mouths. Feel free to try it, if only for the humor of it.

A caption in one of my published articles years ago similarly stated that there's a connection between relaxed hands and a relaxed face, but I didn't actually write that (an editor inserted it). While I surmise that there's a *possible* relationship between hand and facial tensions, I'm inclined to wait for more research on the topic. Rather, in the meantime, I think I can create tension in my face without necessarily creating any tension in my hands, and conversely squeeze my hands without feeling any response in my face.

In general, I've found that attention to the connection between more nearby muscle groups — specifically, the link between hand and arm tension — is a more reliable avenue for improving the skill of relaxation for tennis.

How physical and mental states interact is another worthy topic. Positive body language has been shown to stimulate chemical releases in our brains that correlate with a positive mental outlook. For example, at least one study has indicated that you can improve your mood by smiling for a certain amount of time. You don't even have to actually smile; rather, just manipulate your facial muscles, even by holding a pencil in your teeth.

If modifying body language can affect a person's mood, it may also affect a person's tension. On this topic, substantial research urges us to act in the way that we'd like to be. Richard Wiseman's book, *The As If Principle*, provides a compilation of evidence for how we can alter nearly any part of our lives by *acting as if the desired change was already achieved*. This lends evidence to how we should behave on the tennis court. To be confident and relaxed competitors, we should *behave as if* we're confident and relaxed while competing — even (or especially) if we aren't yet. This has very encouraging implications for our between-point rituals. Our rituals should entail acting how we'd like to be, so that we truly become that (see Chapter 16 On the Habit of Relaxation).

Many players turn to professional coaches for help with excess tension. Unfortunately, one of our challenges related to tension is that we often have difficulty sharing information about it. I once witnessed a coach completely ignore a young player who asked about it. (That player has since completed a PhD in psychology!) While the coach's utter inattention was extreme, his discomfort was understandable. Teaching is usually most comfortable when the topics are straightforward to demonstrate and evaluate, like when a follow-through is taught in the standard way (see Chapter 12 on the Follow-Through), and it's considerably more challenging when the topic is somewhat amorphous, like relaxation.

In 2007, I wrote an article for tennis teaching and coaching professionals on relaxing the hands and arms entitled, "The Most Under-Taught Aspect of Tennis."

Prior to publishing it, I couldn't find any other tennis article related to the topic. If teachers and coaches were not conveying any information on the topic, why would anyone else ever think about it? As a sign of progress, the value of relaxation now gets mentioned here and there, but still largely lacks the attention it deserves. Many players still have no idea that hand and arm tension matters. Though the article was received well and seemed to make a difference by encouraging and emboldening some knowledgeable teachers and coaches to start thinking about and mentioning relaxation, the truth is that the topic is *still* the most under-taught aspect of tennis.

Given the vast resources on relaxation that now generally exist outside of tennis, how you pursue progress from here can vary widely beyond this book, providing for a lifetime of interesting exploration ahead. Skills that can be applied broadly in our lives can also likely be applied specifically to tennis — and vice versa. In this way, the concepts you apply to address tension in your tennis will, in all likelihood, also help you in other areas of your life. General awareness of tension, your ability to alter tension, and your ability to adjust your expectations in relation to tension can become among the most important skills in your life.

Ultimately, one of the best reasons to do anything is to help people, and the hope of this book is to help people to play tennis. This is in part because tennis is so enjoyable, but also because tennis is conducive to living longer and healthier lives.*

As mentioned at the very beginning of this book, for all the people who try tennis for the first time in a typical year, roughly the same number quit. A significant contributing factor is what this book attempts to address: excessive physical strain that hampers control and power, increases fatigue, hinders improvement, and, worst of all, elevates the risk for injury. Most tennis injuries are caused by faulty technique and unnecessary strain; nearly every day I see people playing in a way that both limits their ability to improve and also may cause (or has already caused) injury. For every current player with such issues, there are certainly many more who've already quit for the same reasons.

Decades of experience has led me to conclude that tennis is more appealing, and accordingly more conducive to regular play, when relaxation is emphasized as a primary fundamental of the game. Relinquishing excess tension and strain makes striking the ball more enjoyable and less injurious. Players can feel smooth and graceful and still get a ton of exercise. All of this can be achieved, as top professionals demonstrate, while still allowing, and in fact increasing, chances to win.

---

*Based on a study that tracked over 8,500 people for up to 25 years, playing tennis is one of the best things that you can do for a chance to increase your lifespan — roughly 9.7 years, almost an additional decade! And it isn't just the exercise. Tennis added to average longevity more than any other activity tracked. Cycling added an average of 3.7 years, swimming 3.4, and jogging 3.2. https://www.mayoclinicproceedings.org/article/S0025-6196%2818%2930538-X/fulltext

If the fundamental skill of relaxation is increasingly promoted for tennis players, more new players will be attracted to the game, and many current players will be able to play for more years. Greater attention to relaxation can enhance an individual's overall game and health, and, at the same time, invigorate the sport itself.

www.ingramcontent.com/pod-product-compliance
Ingram Content Group UK Ltd.
Pitfield, Milton Keynes, MK11 3LW, UK
UKHW041641190726
13854UKWH00006B/2642